Dr Bo's

100
Simple Tips

Keeping Your Home Clean and Green

by Phyllis Stylianou

Keeping Your Home Clean and Green

Published by JoJo Publishing
'Yarra's Edge'
2203/80 Lorimer Street
Docklands VIC 3008
Australia
Email: jo-media@bigpond.net.au or visit www.jojopublishing.com

National Library of Australia
Cataloguing in publication data

        Stylianou, Phyllis.
        Keeping Your Home Clean and Green.

      ISBN 9780980369847 (pbk.).

      1. Home economics. 2. House cleaning. 3. Green products.
      I. Title. (Series : Drongo's simple tips).

    648.5

Text by Phyllis Stylianou
Designed by Rob Ryan
Printed in China by Everbest Printing Company, LTD.

Contents

Introduction

Who's got time to make environmentally-friendly cleaning products, keep on top of the housework to make sure it doesn't build up, sort rubbish and make compost? The answer? No one. In a perfect world you would finish work at five, be home by ten past, and cook dinner while the kids played quietly and then went tamely to bed at 8.30 pm (after doing their homework and having a bath without tears and arguments). Friends and rellies would drop by on the week-end to relax in your tidy house and impeccable garden while the children politely handed around cool drinks and home-made cakes.

Unfortunately, in the real world, there are never enough hours in the day, the kids will always behave like ratbags (especially in front of visitors) and you tend to feel as though you're under a constant state of siege. So who wouldn't be tempted to chuck all the rubbish in the same bin and buy every whiz bang chemical in the supermarket? How do you save the planet and your sanity? The answer is simple. Don't. That is, don't try to do everything at once. This book has 100 simple tips to keep your home clean AND green. Each tip is quick and easy to take on by itself. Pick one and use it. You'll be surprised what a difference it makes. Then keep changing one thing a week. Most of all – have fun doing it! Being eco-conscious doesn't mean you also have to be boring about it.

Get rid of the problem

Okay, you've made the decision to stay clean the green way. Now for the really hard step – getting rid of all your chemicals. You'll be surprised how attached you've become to that dishwashing liquid, so harden your heart, grit your teeth, and go systematically through every cupboard in the kitchen, bathroom and laundry (don't forget under the tub!). Don't wimp out now! Put everything in a cardboard box (or three) and call your local council. They'll be able to advise you about the nearest household chemical cleanout drop-off centre. Never ever put chemicals in the bin. There's no point saving the environment at your place if you're destroying it somewhere else as part of landfill.

The clean green shopping list

Now comes the fun bit (for the girls anyway!). It's time to hit the shops and spend some money – but nowhere near as much as you usually spend on those chemical cleaners. These natural ingredients for eco-friendly cleaning solutions go a long way. So make the most of your spending spree, as you won't be doing this again for quite some time. Here's what you'll need:

- Bicarb soda (sodium bicarbonate)
- Borax
- Eucalyptus oil
- White vinegar
- Washing soda
- Methylated spirits
- Cloudy ammonia
- Beeswax
- Lemons
- Pure soap
- Salt
- Olive oil
- Cloves
- Steel wool
- Lavender, peppermint and rose essential oils

Now head home with your goodies and prepare to turn your pantry into a cleaning cupboard!

If you really can't do without them ...

All right, we understand! It's hard to give up all your beloved cleaners at once. If you really MUST keep using some of your chemical 'friends', at least use them sparingly. For a start, minimise temptation by buying less (your bank balance will thank you). Before you hit the shops, check what you've already got in the cupboard. (A cleanout under my laundry tub once revealed six bottles of toilet cleanser and no fewer than 15 bottles of disinfectant in varying states of emptiness. Hubby hit the roof!) Then make a list of what you need, but first ask yourself if there's a safer solution in that fabulous green cleaning kit you've put together.

Safer shopping

You're in the supermarket. You're determined. Your toilet bowl can't possibly be germ-free without chemicals to kill off the nasties. It's okay. We believe you. (We believe that you believe it's true!) Seriously though, it's pretty hard to throw off a lifetime of exposure to ads designed to make us believe that our homes are havens for billions of nasties waiting to attack our loved ones. The same ads push the message that only chemicals are powerful enough to kill those germs and keep us safe. It's convincing stuff. But arm yourself with a bit of knowledge, and it'll be easier to resist. Read the labels. Be particularly wary of products containing nitrogen and phosphorus. Look for labels that read 'no phosphorus' or 'phosphate-free'. Check if it's biodegradable. Above all, if you see the words 'hazardous', 'caution' or 'danger' due to a product's toxicity or potential to cause other health problems, avoid it. The germs it kills are probably safer.

Green cleaning kit

Elbow grease is the number one green cleaning tool. But let's face it – those are words none of us want to hear. Besides, you can't apply your fabulous home-made lotions and potions with your bare hands! And the harder your cleaning tools work, the easier your cleaning products can take it. So put together this basic green cleaning tool kit:

- Microfibre cloths
- Scourer
- Rubber squeegee
- Plastic measuring spoon
- Old toothbrushes
- Fly swat
- Soap shaker
- Paint scraper
- Spray bottles
- Old cotton singlets, t-shirts and towels
- Old cotton or wool socks
- Steel wool
- Long and short handled scrubbing brushes
- Plastic buckets
- Glass jars with lids

Microfibre cloths

Speaking of microfibre cloths – what on earth are they? Yes, they're synthetic, but they've earned a place in the green cleaning kit because these handy little devices are able to pick up dirt without the need for chemical cleansers. They're more absorbent than natural fibre cloths, don't cause scratching, are easy to use and can be washed and re-used. There are microfibre cloths to suit every household cleaning task, but start with an all-purpose cloth and build up your collection from there. Just make sure you don't wash them with fabric softener as it coats the fibres and makes the cloths useless.

The natural stain remover kit

Everyone loves a kit. So here's another one for you. Put those boy scouts to shame and be prepared for any stain emergency with the following ingredients, then look for the recipes later in this book.

- Bicarb soda
- Borax
- Cloudy ammonia
- Cream of tartar
- Epsom salts
- Eucalyptus oil
- Hydrogen peroxide
- Lemon juice
- Methylated spirits
- Phosphate-free colourless dishwashing liquid
- Pure soap or soap flakes
- Salt
- Soda water
- Vegetable glycerine
- Washing soda
- White vinegar

So you don't want to make your own?

A number of companies make green cleaning products based or organic substances, such as orange oil. You'll find many of them on supermarket shelves (look for the Environmental Choice logo), while others are available via the internet. Check out www.todae.com.au, www.planetarkdirect.com and www.biome.com.au. You'll find everything from laundry bleach and toilet cleaner to dishwasher powder and organic cotton cloth nappies.

You don't even want to do it yourself?

Relax – literally! There are professional house cleaners out there who specialise in using eco-friendly products. You can even have your car and wheelie bins washed for you by businesses that specialise in using environmentally-friendly products, and are licensed for water use. The internet is your best friend in this situation. Just jump online, punch in 'green cleaning' and check out the services on offer.

VOCs

Poo, what's that smell? Before you reach for the can of air freshener (but after you check bub's nappy), stop and think. (You DID get rid of that can, didn't you?) Your nose is sending you an important message. It could be dust (in which case, reach for your new arsenal of eco cleaning equipment) or, worse, it could be VOCs. Volatile Organic Compounds are fumes released from carpets, furnishings, cleaning products, paints, plastics, air fresheners pesticides and aerosol sprays. And the effects they have on us are scary, ranging from skin, eye and throat irritations to headaches and nausea. Some are even known or thought to cause cancer. These are not smells you want to mask with fragrance – these are smells you want to eliminate. The best way to do this is to use natural products and materials as much as possible. You can even buy VOC-free paint. As for that air freshener, try one or all of the alternatives outlined on pages 11, 12 and 13.

Fresh air tip
1: ventilate

Yep, that's it! Open the windows and doors. Let Mother Nature do some of the work for you. (That's what mums are for!) Not only will the stink go out, the fresh air will help prevent some other nasty problems, like mould and mildew build-up, foggy windows and damp bedding and soft furnishings. And there's nothing like a bit of sunshine to warm up the house. While you're at it, remember to take a few deep lungfuls of fresh air yourself. See, you're feeling better already!

Fresh air tip
2: choose natural flooring and furnishings

Give synthetics a big miss and go for natural materials like wool or goat hair carpets with felt underlays. Rubber and linoleum look hip in the kitchen, bathroom and laundry. And look for cotton, linen or hessian soft furnishings, with latex or natural fibre cushions to top it all off. If you're building your home, choose green building materials such as recycled or sustainably-harvested timber flooring. Or why not go with bamboo or engineered timber? The bonus is that natural products last longer, look and feel better – and keep you and the planet healthy.

Fresh air tip
3: bring in the pot plants!

No, that's not an invitation to start growing wacky tobaccy in the spare room! But indoor plants like peace lily, Boston fern, English ivy and gerberas are just some of the green machines that can help purify the air in your home. They literally suck toxins out of the air and replace them with fresh, life-giving oxygen. And they look great! While you're at it, get rid of those abominable fake flowers you paid a fortune for – they're contributing to the VOCs in the house.

Sort yourself out

You've probably heard of the three-bin compost system – what about the three-bin kitchen system? Better yet, three small buckets with lids instead of one big stinky bin. Use one for cans, bottles and other recyclables, one for food scraps and paper that can be composted and the third (lined with one of the plastic shopping bags you'll still inevitably pick up somewhere) for the rest. No need to waste money buying buckets either. If you have old plastic toy boxes, or big plastic storage boxes, you can use them instead. Or if you're friendly with the owner of your local takeaway or deli, ask them if they'll save you some of the large plastic buckets their fetta, mayonnaise and yoghurt come in.

Recycling

Recycling doesn't just mean tossing cans, papers and bottles in the council-provided bin. (Although it's a good way to help the planet!) It also means finding new uses for previously useless items. Jars are handy for storing some of the fabulous cleaning lotions and potions we'll be making later, and old clothes (including stockings) make great cleaning rags. Even better, because you're not using chemical cleaners, the cloths can be tossed together in the washing machine and reused.

More is less

That's right, clean little and often. You won't need to use as much natural OR chemical product if you can keep on top of the dirt. Try tidying up as you go and it'll be less daunting than facing a huge mess at the end of the day – or week. And speaking of weeks, try to establish a minimum weekly routine to prevent the grease and grime building up. Put this to-do list on your fridge and tick things off as you go. Each of them only takes a few minutes. Try doing just one thing each day, and there'll be nothing to stop you heading out to enjoy yourself on the weekend.

- Vacuum and dust rooms
- Shake the door mats
- Wipe over the fridge and kitchen cupboard doors
- Wipe the stove and wash the grill tray
- Wash the bins
- Sweep the verandahs
- Clean the toilet and wipe down the basin

How do you eat an elephant? Cut it into very small pieces. Same thing goes for cleaning.

Stop the dirt from coming in

Have a shoe-free policy for the family. (Don't extend this to visitors. They might have a foot odour problem that'll have you wishing you'd kept that can of air freshener. Or they may have holes in their socks. Either way, it'll guarantee that you'll lose your friends!) Place a shoe rack at the door and a chair next to it to make taking shoes off easier. Dirt-absorbing mats at all entrances will not only keep the worst offenders outside, they'll save wear and tear on your precious floor coverings.

Reuse or recycle containers

If you do buy some cleaning products, look for the ones that come in refillable containers – that way you won't be contributing too much to landfill. Other products are available in biodegradable packaging, such as recycled cardboard or paper that will break down in the compost heap. If worst comes to worst, and it's not recyclable or refillable, ask yourself if you can put the container to some other use.

Be prepared

The greatest temptation to reach for the chemical cleaners comes when you're busy, there's too much work to get through and that ready-made stuff is sitting in the cupboard calling your name. 'Pick me, pick me,' it cries. 'I know you're busy, I can help you. Come on, you know you want to use me!' That's when you reach for your new arsenal of cleaners that you have made up, ready to go at a moment's notice. They're stored in spray bottles and old glass jam jars (what better excuse to eat jam sandwiches!) and just as easy to grab, along with the bucket of rags you've got alongside them in the cupboard. Give your halo an extra shine with bicarb paste and let those chemical cleaners grit their teeth in frustration!

Bicarb cleaner

Told you you'd be using a lot of this stuff. In a jar, mix one teaspoon of bicarb, one teaspoon of pure soap flakes, a squeeze of lemon or dash of white vinegar and one cup of water. Put the lid on and shake the jar until the soap has dissolved, then pour the mix into a spray bottle. This is a good general purpose cleaner for anywhere in the home – just spray it on and wipe off with a kitchen sponge. And yes, you can keep it in the cupboard. (Don't forget to pop a label on it so you know what you're grabbing next time.)

Vinegar cleaner

No, it won't make the house stink, we promise! Vinegar is a mild acid that neutralises grease and soap residue. And what you don't use for cleaning, you can pour on your salad! Combine two cups of white vinegar, one cup of water and 25 drops of eucalyptus oil in a spray bottle. Shake well, spray onto a soft damp cloth and rub onto sinks, timber surfaces and plastic finishes such as fridge shelves and telephones. This is a great one to remove grease and dirt and, best of all, there's no need to rinse!

Lavender disinfectant

Add 25 drops of lavender essential oil to two tablespoons of methylated spirits or vodka in a clean, dry bottle. (What you do with the rest of the vodka is up to you!) Leave it for 24 hours then add 500 mL of distilled water. Pour it into a spray bottle, shake thoroughly and use it to keep bathroom surfaces safe and smelling sweet. It's fantastic to spray on bed linen during ironing (if you have that much energy!). This also makes a lovely gift idea. Pour it into a pretty glass spray bottle, add a sprig of lavender to make it look attractive (and increase the potency of the lavender) then label it 'Lavender Water' using a little card attached to the neck of the bottle with a piece of lavender ribbon. Your girlfriends will love you!

Lemon juice bleach

Behind every successful blonde is a cup of lemon juice! This is a great natural bleach, and not just for hair. It disinfects and inhibits the growth of mould – not to mention smells a heck of a lot better than the commercial stuff. It even removes stubborn mildew stains from shower curtains. Just rub the area with lemon juice and allow it to dry in the sun. And if there's anything left over – well, you've always wondered how you'd look as a blonde, haven't you?

Salt disinfectant

If you've ever been to the beach with even a tiny graze somewhere, you'll have felt the sting of the salt water as it goes to work, killing any little germs that may be present. And every kid knows to brace themselves when mum sees an open wound of any description – there's a bottle of lukewarm salty water headed their way whether they like it or not! So if it's good enough for first aid, it's got to be good enough for wiping down kitchen and bathroom surfaces, especially when mixed with vinegar. Mixed into a paste with just a little water, it makes a handy mild abrasive too.

Tea-tree and eucalyptus oil surface wipe

Tea-tree oil is a natural disinfectant and soothing balm (ask anyone who's ever had a lip wax or electrolysis!) Eucalyptus oil comes from the eucalyptus gum tree – just ask yourself, when was the last time you saw a koala with stained fur? Add a few drops of either of these oils to hot water and you've got yourself a strong-smelling disinfectant surface wipe. (Who knows, you may even find yourself attracting a family of koalas to move in!)

Soap and borax cleaner

Now we're starting to bring out the big guns. When it comes to green cleaning, borax is one of the tough guys on the block. Stains see it coming and bolt for the hills. But a word to the wise: just because something's natural, doesn't necessarily mean it's harmless. This mineral salt is poisonous when swallowed, so don't leave it lying around where the kids might find it. As a cleaner though, it's fantastic. Mix two teaspoons of borax with one heaped teaspoon of pure soap flakes and three cups of water. Store it in an airtight spray bottle (away from the kids) and use it to clean bench tops and other surfaces.

Lemon cream cleanser

When you think essential oils, lemon doesn't always spring immediately to mind. But it's great stuff that leaves a fresh, tangy smell around the house. Squirt phosphate-free liquid detergent into half a cup of bicarb until it forms a soft paste. Add one teaspoon of vegetable glycerine and several drops of lemon essential oil. Use as a slightly abrasive cleaner for baths, basins, benches and cook tops. Just apply it with a damp sponge, then rinse it off.

Glass cleaner

Dilute half a cup of vinegar in two litres of water then spray it onto glass, mirrors and tiles for a streak-free finish. Soap scum is easy to remove by mixing two parts salt with one part vinegar. Rub the mixture on with a cloth, then rinse and allow the glass to dry. Last but not least, admire your clean, green self in the mirror as you shower. If you fancy a fog-free view, wipe it over with glycerine or a thin film of shaving cream, then buff with a soft cloth.

Laundry powder

The best thing about making your own washing powder (apart from the price), is you can use the grey water on the garden. Talk about value for money! Just put half a cup of washing soda crystals in a plastic bag (yet another chance to recycle) and crush them with a rolling pin. (Make sure you wash the pin thoroughly before using it on your husband again!) Mix with one cup of finely grated pure soap, half a cup of salt, half a cup of borax and half a cup of bicarb. Store the mixture in an airtight box or jar, ready for wash day. Use one tablespoon for a small load, one and a half tablespoons for a medium load and two tablespoons for a large load. Dissolve the powder in a jug of hot water if you have a top loader. If you have a front loader, dissolve it in a small amount of hot water, then add to the dispenser.

Fabric softener

Going green doesn't mean you have to put up with crunchy towels! Add one cup of white vinegar to the washing machine during the rinse cycle (or two tablespoons to the fabric softener dispenser for front loaders). If it's the pretty smell that you crave, never fear! Just add a few drops of lavender, lemon, rose or eucalyptus oil to the vinegar. If you can't get past the idea of putting vinegar in the wash (trust us, it doesn't make the clothes stink!) use a quarter of a cup of bicarb with a few drops of essential oil instead.

Pre-wash stain remover

Get the most out of that fabulous washing powder you've just made by treating stains before you put your clothes in the machine. How? Glad you asked! Add half a cup of borax to 500 mL of water and pour it into a spray bottle. Then spray it on the stains the same way you would if you were using the bought stuff. If you still can't shift the beetroot off your favourite shirt, it's time to pull out the big guns. Mix three tablespoons of mild, colour-free dishwashing liquid, three tablespoons of vegetable glycerine and 375 mL of water in a spray bottle. Squirt it on, wait 15 to 30 minutes, then wash away the pain (sorry, stain).

Brighter whites

Do you love the idea of snow-white linen and clothes, but can't stand the stench of bleach and the damage it eventually does to the fabric? Try adding half a cup of borax to hot washing water instead! (The temperature must be higher than 60°C for the borax to work.) Or, try using some good, old-fashioned washing blue in the final rinse! (Blue bags are available from the supermarket, and are pretty handy for bee stings too.) If you've got blue towels, toss them in with your white sheets for the same effect.

Nappies

If you've got the time (and energy) to go the cloth nappy route, you'll know that poo creates stains – big time. Keep your bub's eco-friendly bot looking bright and white by soaking them (the nappies, not the baby) overnight in a bucket of hot water with a cup of borax. (Don't forget to empty the offending stuff into the toilet first!) Wash the nappies as usual and add a cup of vinegar to the rinse. If you're really keen, it's also possible to buy nappies made from hemp. They're washable and incredibly soft.

Eucalyptus wool wash

Nanna couldn't just nip down the shops for a bottle of wool wash every time a blanket or jumper got dirty. So how did she keep them soft and fluffy? With two cups of soap flakes, half a cup of methylated spirits and 25 mL of eucalyptus oil mixed together in a jar. If you add two tablespoons to a litre of warm washing water your woollens will feel great, smell fabulous and keep moths at bay when they're in the wardrobe. (They don't call koalas cuddly for nothing!)

Ironing

Remove scorch marks by soaking the affected area in pure lemon juice for half an hour. Rinse in warm water and dry in the sun. The lemon juice and sunshine have a natural bleaching effect. If you want to avoid ironing altogether (or at least minimise it), smooth and fold your clothes as your take them off the line. Woollen clothes can be hung in the bathroom while you're having a shower. The steam will cause the creases to drop out. (This is an especially useful excuse for not running the exhaust fan on those cold winter nights!)

Revive your clothes

There's nothing more embarrassing than the yellow stains that perspiration leaves on the underarm area of clothes. But there's no need to consign your favourite white top to the rag bag just yet. Just rub the stains with a paste of vegetable glycerine and cream of tartar. Leave it to work its magic for 24 hours then wash as normal. You can also spruce up your old jeans by washing them with a new pair. It's the cheapest, easiest dye job around.

Hand washing

Many 'dry-clean only' items, including silks and woollens, can be hand washed in lukewarm or cold water. Pure soap flakes are kind on your hands and clothes, as is that fabulous home-made wool wash! If you feel something really should be dry-cleaned only, try spot cleaning to get more wears in between trips to the cleaners. Best of all, try not washing at all! (Well, not as often, anyway.) Does that skirt or pair of pants really need to be washed after every wear? Probably not. Try hanging it outside to air for the day instead.

Machine washing

Make the most of wash day by sorting everything into loads. That way you can choose the best cycle and achieve the best result. (You'll also avoid accidental dye jobs.) Treat grime and stains beforehand by soaking overnight or using home-made pre-wash stain remover. Above all, remember that hot water doesn't necessarily mean a cleaner wash. In fact, it can damage or shrink some delicate fabrics. The cold stuff can't do any harm and saves energy (and money).

Bed linen

Sheets, pillowcases, doona covers and mattress protectors can be washed in the machine, but pillows can be hand washed in soapy water or wool wash, then dried outside in the shade. (Turn and shake them frequently to keep them soft and fluffy.) And avoid the need to drag your doona to the dry cleaners by airing it on the clothesline to keep it fresh. If it gets stained, try spot cleaning. Most can be washed if necessary. Knead it in warm soapy water or wool wash in the bath. Rinse well and lay it flat on the grass (with an old sheet underneath) to dry. Remember to turn and shake it frequently.

Towels and tea towels

Soften new towels and remove any chemicals left over from the manufacturing process by soaking them in a tub of water with a handful of bicarb. Then wash as usual and add a cup of vinegar to the final rinse. Damp towels are a breeding ground for bacteria, so machine wash them frequently. If they get scratchy, try softening them by soaking overnight in a bucket of water with half a cup of Epsom salts. Don't rinse the solution out. And look like a pro as you peg them out by giving each towel a good shake – it fluffs up the pile and keeps it soft. Soak dirty tea towels overnight in a solution of two tablespoons of cream of tartar per litre of boiling water. Then wash as usual. If they're really greasy, add two tablespoons of borax to the washing water (this will disinfect them as well).

Blankets

Very dirty, non-woollen blankets can be soaked for 20 minutes before washing in warm water on the machine's gentle cycle. Woollen blankets should be hand washed in warm (never hot) water but can be put in the machine if it has a wool cycle. Never rub, wring or tumble dry a woollen blanket. Gently squeeze it out then roll it in several towels to remove the excess water. Dry it flat, or draped over several lines on the clothesline.

Tubs and machines

Clean surfaces with bicarb sprinkled on a damp cloth – but use it sparingly as it can scratch. Wipe stainless steel tubs with a moist microfibre cloth then dry with an absorbent cloth. Spray sink stains with white vinegar then wipe clean. Use bicarb on stubborn stains and dry with an absorbent cloth. Wipe washing machines and tumble dryers with a cloth moistened with white vinegar or bicarb.

General bathroom cleaning

Wipe the toilet brush handle, bath and shower and all fittings after each use. Clean hard water marks with vinegar or lemon juice. Remove tough stains by soaking a cloth in vinegar then letting the cloth sit on the mark for an hour before wiping the area clean. Keep bench tops and basins dry to discourage the growth of mould. Wash bath mats every week and hang them over the side of the shower or bath to dry or, better yet, in the sun for natural sterilisation.

Toilet cleaner

Step one: ask everyone in the house if they need to go to the loo. Step 2: make them go anyway! That's because this cleaner needs an hour or two to work its magic. Okay, now you're ready to clean inside the toilet bowl. Just sprinkle the damp surface with one cup of borax, then spray it with a quarter of a cup of vinegar. Leave it for an hour or two then scrub with a toilet brush and flush. Disinfect the bowl quickly and easily between cleans by adding a few drops of pine oil or tea-tree oil.

Toilet air freshener

Let's clear the air. We all know that an open window sometimes just isn't enough when it comes to getting rid of toilet odours. And if you know there's someone else waiting to go in, well who wouldn't reach for the spray can? But there are a few things you can do to avoid embarrassment. Try lighting an aromatherapy oil burner, candle or even a match (no, the place won't explode, we promise!). If you prefer to have an actual spray bottle ready for yourself and guests to use, then just keep a small water spray bottle near the toilet, filled with water and a few drops of lemon, tea-tree or lavender essential oil. Place a label on the bottle that says 'Air freshener – shake then spray'. Your guests will be most appreciative!

Mould fighter

Prevention is better than cure when it comes to mould.
Fresh air is free and requires no more effort to use than
opening the window. Turning on the exhaust fan doesn't hurt
either. (We'll forgive you if you conveniently forget this one in
winter!) You can also stop mould from forming by treating
bathroom surfaces with a mixture of two teaspoons of borax
and one cup of white vinegar. Spray or wipe it on and leave it
for half an hour before wiping it off.

Wet areas

Wash the basin, bath and shower recess with white vinegar or bicarb. Wipe fibreglass baths and shower recesses with a solution of half a cup of washing soda in half a bucket of hot water. Clean stains from shower curtains with bicarb or vinegar on a damp cloth. Rinse clean then dry in the sun. Wash shower curtains regularly in hot, soapy water then dry in the sun. Remove stains made by dripping taps with a paste of borax and lemon juice. Just rub it over the mark, leave it for a few minutes then wipe clean.

Spray stopper

Here's a great hint from my grandad – 93-years-young and a housekeeping guru since Nan passed away. Stop liquid cleaners from disappearing down the drain too quickly by laying an old singlet or t-shirt across the bottom of the shower, bath or sink (including the plug hole). The liquid will be trapped on the surface and you can leave it there to soak for as long as you like. When you're ready, remove the rag and clean as normal.

Shower screens

Reduce soap build-up by wiping shower screens daily with a microfibre cloth. To remove soap that has already built up over time, rub shower screens with bicarb paste on a scourer, then rinse and clean with a cloth moistened with vinegar. Wipe dry with an absorbent cloth. Shower screens should also be cleaned regularly with damp cloth and vinegar, then dried with an absorbent cloth.

Mirror mirror

Clean mirrors with hot water and a microfibre cloth then dry with an absorbent cloth. Alternatively, spray mirrors with vinegar, clean then wipe dry with an absorbent cloth. Wipe mirrors with eucalyptus oil to prevent fogging.

Tile style

Clean the grot from grout with bicarb and a toothbrush. (The one from the cleaning kit, not the one you're still using!), then rinse then dry with a cloth. Remove difficult stains with Epsom salts and a toothbrush, rinse with warm water or vinegar and hot water then dry with a cloth. Wipe the tiles regularly with vinegar and water to deter dirt and mould build-up.

Toilet training

Clean the outside of the loo regularly with hot soapy water. A good way to keep the inside of the bowl clean is to pour a cup of hot water and vinegar into the toilet bowl at night then clean with a toilet brush in the morning. Rub built-up stains with bicarb. Disinfect the toilet bowl and seat by spraying them with vinegar and wiping clean with a damp cloth.

General kitchen cleaning

Try to maintain high standards of cleanliness (i.e. don't leave food lying around) to deter cockroaches, mice and ants. Clean all surfaces with hot water and vinegar and use bicarb on extra dirty areas. Wipe up food spills straight away (you'll only have to scrub them off later anyway!) Clean plastic chopping boards with hot soapy water and scour timber ones with salt paste. Aluminium saucepans should be cleaned with steel wool and hot soapy water (never bicarb) while stainless steel utensils can be sprinkled with bicarb and scoured with steel wool. Keep your cupboards clean and pest-free by wiping up food spills immediately, cleaning out the pantry monthly and the utensils cupboards annually. Use hot soapy water and keep the doors open while they dry.

Scouring paste

Ah bicarb! Every nanna's favourite cleaner and heartburn remedy. Hope you bought a big box of it on your shopping trip, because this stuff is an eco-cleaning staple. It would be great never to scour anything (who needs the hassle?). But if you do, this is the best stuff for the job. Mix four tablespoons of bicarb with one tablespoon of water to form a stiff paste. It's as simple as that. So simple, in fact, why would you even bother making a batch in advance? Use a damp sponge to apply it to sinks, oven doors, cook tops and even the inside of stained mugs, then buff off the residue with a dry cloth.

Saucepan cleaner

You've burnt the bolognaise again! Dinner may be ruined, but at least your aluminium saucepan can be saved. Place two cups of cream of tartar, two teaspoons of vinegar and one litre of water in the offending pot. Boil it for 10 minutes and, hey presto, your pot's sparkling like new. Pity the same can't be said for the bolognaise. You could also try removing the scorched food remains by boiling an onion in the saucepan.

Detergent

Remember Madge the nail lady? 'You're soaking in it.' 'Dishwashing liquid?' her client exclaims in horror. While we wouldn't recommend soaking your fingers in this one (or any other detergent for that matter) it's still a nice, mild dishwashing liquid. Put one and a half cups of pure soap flakes and three quarters of a cup of water in a saucepan and bring it to the boil. Reduce the heat and stir until the mixture is smooth. Remove from the heat and stir in one and a half cups of washing soda until blended. Add one and a half cups of vinegar and a few drops of lemon essential oil, then store in a sealed bottle. Use a teaspoon or two in hot water for sparkling dishes. Madge would be proud!

Drain strain

If you've ever put a new sink in the kitchen, you'll have seen how putrid the bottom of the u-bend in the drainpipe can get. Not only does the sight put you well and truly off your dinner, it can eventually lead to blockages and a visit from the plumber. (Never good if you value your money!) Try to avoid the problem by placing a sink sieve in the drain hole and giving the drain an occasional clean by pouring a cup of washing soda down the sink followed by boiling water. Alternatively, use a handful of bicarb followed by half a cup of vinegar.

Dish plan

When you're washing the dishes, use pure soap and make your glasses sparkle by adding a small amount of vinegar to the rinse water. Save water by rinsing the dishes in a bowl of clean water rather than running them under the tap. Clean stained tea and coffee mugs with fine steel wool or bicarb on a damp cloth. Last but not least, get rid of the invisible nasties lurking in your sink cleaning cloths and tea towels by drying them in direct sunlight – it's a natural steriliser.

Grease trap

Ever peeked on top of the fridge or kitchen cupboards, seen the greasy layer of grime, shuddered and walked away? Cleaning the toilet bowl with bare hands and a toothbrush is more appealing than trying to get rid of that stuff. So don't! Stop the sludge before it starts. Cut pieces of thick paper or newspaper to fit on top of those high places where cooking grease settles and gathers dust. Change it twice a year and you'll never need to scrub up there again!

Floor plan

The kitchen must have one of the dirtiest floors in the house. Forget the accidental crumb and coffee spills – what about the peas and broccoli that are surreptitiously dropped under the table at dinner time. (And they thought you wouldn't notice!) Sweep the kitchen floor, then mop it with a cup of vinegar in half a bucket of hot water. Spray extra dirty patches with vinegar, leave for 10 minutes then wipe them clean. Scuff marks can be removed with eucalyptus oil.

The oven

Step one is to stop putting off this job. Step two is to do it regularly so the grease doesn't build up. Seriously, you're only making a rod for your own back! Here's the drill: wipe the oven clean with a soapy cloth while it's still warm and, if it's really dirty, use some bicarb on a damp cloth. Bicarb is also good for cleaning glass oven doors, so while you're at it, give them a going over too. That way you can see the roast burning. Cook tops can be sprayed with white vinegar and wiped clean.

Sinks and surfaces

Clean your bench tops with some bicarb on a damp cloth
– but use it sparingly as it can scratch. Wipe stainless steel
sinks with a microfibre cloth then dry them with an
absorbent cloth (remember your bag of rags!). This will
remove the damp environment that bacteria love to breed
in. Sink stains can be sprayed with white vinegar then wiped
clean. Use bicarb on a damp cloth for the stubborn marks.

Whitegoods

Use vinegar on a damp cloth (bicarb if the surface is very dirty), then wipe it with a dry cloth. Wash inside the fridge with warm soapy water or bicarb on a damp cloth if it's really dirty. Deodorise inside the fridge by wiping it with vanilla essence. It's a good idea to give the inside of the fridge a good clean out every shopping day, before you put the groceries away. If you don't, old food and food spills will eventually go mouldy and cause a health hazard.

Windows

Sprinkle vinegar on a damp cloth to wipe the glass then dry
it with an absorbent cloth. Wash really dirty windows with
hot soapy water and rinse using vinegar mixed with water
before drying with an absorbent cloth. Why not put that fabulous squeegee you bought to use by cleaning the
outside of the windows at the same time? Don't be like
Queen Victoria, who often had to guess what the weather
was like outside because her servants couldn't be bothered
coordinating the outside window washers with the
inside ones!

Hard floor cleaner

(Don't use this one on timber floors.)

You can't really make this one up in advance, but how much harder is it to pour three simple things into a bucket of hot water than one stinky chemical? Mix one tablespoon of liquid soap, a quarter of a cup of white vinegar and a quarter of a cup of washing soda with three litres of hot water in a bucket. (Washing soda can damage the skin, so wear gloves.) Mop the floor then rinse it with clean water.

Carpet stain foam

Add two cups of pure soap flakes, half a cup of methylated spirits and 25 mL of eucalyptus oil to a jar and shake well. (Yes, it's meant to be thick.) Seal the jar and store until you need it, then pray you don't need it. If your prayers go unanswered, here's what you do: mix two or three tablespoons of mixture with one litre of very hot water and whisk until suds form. Rub the foam only over the stain and leave for 10 minutes. Wipe away with a sponge dipped in white vinegar then blot dry with a clean cloth rolled into a pad. If the stain is extra stubborn, add a quarter of a cup of washing soda to the hot water and foam mix.

Tiled floors

Vacuum or sweep sealed ceramic tiles, then sponge-mop them with a bucket of water and two cups of vinegar. Marks on glazed tiles can be removed with a bit of bicarb, while unglazed tiles can be rubbed gently with fine steel wool and a bit of bicarb. If you've got crawling bubs and want to make sure the floor is thoroughly cleaned and disinfected, mop it with half a cup of borax dissolved in a bucket of hot water.

Floorboards

My Mum has fond childhood memories of Nan putting wax on the floor then getting her to slide around on a mat made from old rags. Mum had a good time and Nan got the floor polished in record time. If you don't have any obliging toddlers, just sweep unsealed timber floorboards and polish them with a cloth impregnated with linseed oil. Sealed timber should be swept then sponge-mopped with a just a little bit of water, or water and a tiny bit of detergent. If your floor has been oil-finished or coated with polyurethane, wash it with one part methylated spirits to 10 parts hot water then buff it with a dry cloth. If your oil-finished floor has any sticky patches, sprinkle them with flour then wipe with a damp cloth.

Lino and vinyl floors

Mopping with good old fashioned H2O and a little bit of detergent should be enough to get linoleum or vinyl clean most of the time. Just remember to wipe up spills as soon as they happen to prevent stains. If you're not quick enough and there's a mark, use a fine nylon pad and detergent.
Scuff marks are a cinch. Pinch one of the kids' pencil erasers and use it to remove the offending mark. If they're really stubborn (the marks, not the kids) try rubbing the area with a little dishwashing liquid. (Don't forget to wipe it clean with a damp cloth or you could end up testing the floor with your bottom!)

Furniture polish

There's nothing like the smell of beeswax polish in the house. And it's all yours for just a little bit of elbow grease (or wax in this case). Grate 125 mL of beeswax into a heatproof bowl over a saucepan of simmering water. Add 500 mL of raw linseed oil (for dark timber) or olive oil (for pale timber) and stir over the heat for three minutes. Remove from the heat and stir in a teaspoon of lavender or rosemary essential oil. Pour it into a clean jar and allow it to set. To use, scoop a small ball of wax from the jar, place it inside a fine soft cloth and rub it gently over the surface. The trick is not to apply it too thickly, or it will be hard to rub off. Give it half an hour to dry then polish it off.

All purpose metal polish

Try this inexpensive polish to clean brass, copper, bronze, pewter and stainless steel. Combine equal parts of salt and plain flour then add enough vinegar to make a stiff paste. Rub it sparingly on the metal item and allow it to dry for a couple of hours. Rinse it off and polish with a soft cloth. Mixing this one up yourself is just as easy as opening the lid of a commercial metal polish, and let's face it, how often do you clean that stuff anyway?

Brass cleaner

Brass is beautiful – until it becomes tarnished, then it's a blot on your conscience because you haven't cleaned it. The easy, hassle-free answer is 25 grams of citric acid mixed with three litres of hot water. Just place the offending item in the solution and let it soak for five minutes. Give it a gentle scrub with an old toothbrush, rinse it off and dry it. Voila! Your conscience is clear, your brass is clean and it wasn't even hard work.

Silver cleaner

'Scrub-free silver? Impossible!' you say. But there is another way ... line the bottom of a non-metal bucket or large bowl with aluminium foil. Add a tablespoon each of salt and bicarb then fill the bucket with boiling water. Soak washable silver items (not Granddad's fob watch!) in the solution for a couple of hours. All that's left to do is rinse them, dry them off and return them to the display cabinet.

Living rooms and bedrooms

These are the rooms where dust tends to build up on furniture and appliances and toys, books, magazines and other bits and pieces left lying around create a general air of untidiness. Wipe Holland blinds with a vinegar-moistened cloth. Dust Venetians then wipe them wipe a vinegar-moistened cloth. Dust furniture with a microfibre cloth. As for the clutter, try putting everything in a cardboard box early on cleaning day and announce to the family that anything still there that evening will go in the bin. Be prepared to carry out your threat or they'll never take you seriously again.

Computers, TV's and sound systems

These things attract dust like nobody's business. Dust computer keyboards with a microfibre cloth. Remove stubborn dirt with a vinegar-moistened cloth. Dust TV and computer screens with a microfibre cloth. Alternatively, wipe them over with a vinegar-moistened cloth and dry with an absorbent cloth. Dust all other entertainment appliances with a microfibre cloth.

Book nook

Dust off your books at least once a year using a heavy makeup brush on the closed pages. Better yet, read them regularly to reduce dampness and stop the dust from settling. If a book has a musty smell, try placing it in a paper bag with crumpled newspaper. And if you're lucky enough to have anything that's leather bound, clean the covers with a damp cloth. It's sometimes recommended to wipe them over with a little vegetable oil to condition the leather, but only do this if absolutely necessary, as it tends to darken the cover and encourage mould.

Using appliances

It's possible to take green cleaning to the extreme and start using washboards, hand wringers and polishing the floors with beeswax and a rag on your hands and knees – but why on earth would you want to? And let's face it, who's got time anyway? Used properly, appliances can make green cleaning easier, and some are even more eco-friendly than Nan's old washboard! See the following tips for information about using appliances the green way!

Vacuuming

While none of us would want to return to the bad old days of backbreaking housework without modern appliances, there's still a lot to be said for some (not all) of Nan's housekeeping methods. Take, if you will, the carpet sweeper. Still to be found in the mop and broom section of every supermarket, this is a classic way of vacuuming the carpet without wasting electricity. They're a lot lighter than many vacuum cleaners, smaller and (if you ask me) easier to use. Sure, you can whip out the electric model once a month to get the deep down nitty gritty, but for that weekly once over the carpet square, why not give the sweeper a go. Nan'll be proud!

Washing

You could try washing by hand in the laundry tub – but it'd take all weekend, nothing else would get done, and your hands would be red raw at the end of it (as would your temper!) Sure, rinse out your undies in the shower or a bucket of (home-made) soapy water. But these days, your best bet is to take a good long look at your old washing machine. My first washing machine was an abandoned 10 kg top loader my brother-in-law found in a paddock. In an effort to be water-conscious, I put the hose out the laundry window into a 240 litre garbage bin. (Yes, it was empty at the time!) Just one load filled the bin to overflowing. I dutifully used the proceeds of several loads to water the garden – only to kill off nearly every plant over the course of a few weeks. (I didn't realise how much damage phosphates could do.) Thankfully the machine also died after a few months and I bought a AAAA water-rated, four energy star front loader. The water bills went down, the power bills went down, the new plants survived, and I now use phosphate-free, home-made washing powder. Enough said!

Clothes dryers

Blessed as I was with a large backyard and a house with an attic, I scoffed disdainfully as my sisters (both with young families) bought clothes dryers. 'Energy wasters,' I scoffed. 'They should just be more organised.' Then I had a baby. And it rained – for days. Suddenly a tumble dryer seemed like a very good idea indeed! And so they are. Used sparingly. While the kindest thing for the environment, your wallet, and your clothes, is still plenty of fresh air and sunshine, there are occasions when one of these appliances can save your sanity. Just remember to get a model with the maximum number of energy stars and save it for those cold wet winter nights when the baby has wet, dirtied or vomited on every sheet, towel and article of clothing in the house!

Dishwashers

Difficult as this may be to believe, you're actually wasting more water washing up by hand than if you use a dishwasher (provided it's energy- and water-efficient of course). Modern dishwashers can use as little as nine litres of water to wash a whole load (the dishes from an entire day's meals), as opposed to 18 litres to wash the dishes from one meal in the sink. Times three, that's a whopping 54 litres a day before you even think about rinsing!

Barbecues

Clean off as much food residue as possible, then turn the barbecue to high (or choose the Clean Burn setting if you have one). This will burn off any excess fat. While the plate is hot, sprinkle it with salt, leave it to cool then brush clean. The grates and hotplate can be scrubbed with a mixture of bicarb and water, wiped clean and dried with a cloth. When the barbecue is clean, apply a coat of canola oil to the grates and hotplate to prevent rust.

Garden tools

Clean garden tools every time you use them and carry out regular maintenance. Wipe timber handles regularly with a mixture of one part boiled linseed oil and one part natural turpentine while the metal parts should be wiped with a damp rag dipped in linseed oil. Wipe vegetable oil on the clean metal underside of your lawnmower to prevent dirt build-up.

Outdoor furniture

Most types of outdoor furniture can be scrubbed with a nylon-bristled brush and warm water with a squirt of phosphate-free dishwashing liquid. Wipe clean with an unsoiled, wet rag. Timber furniture should be allowed to dry, sanded lightly then oiled with two cups of raw linseed oil mixed with half a cup of natural turps. Aluminium furniture should be wiped with warm water and a dash of vinegar. Make sure cane and wicker furniture is kept dry, or it will go mouldy. Brush the dirt off canvas furniture regularly and give it the occasional wash with clean cold water. Bird poo and mildew stains can be treated with a paste of salt and lemon juice. Leave it in the sun until the stain disappears, then rinse off. Stubborn stains can be treated with bicarb paste.

Play equipment

Cover the sandpit when it's not in use to keep it free of animal droppings and rubbish. Clean a dirty wading pool with a solution of a quarter of a cup of bicarb and four litres of water. Swings and slides should be scrubbed regularly with warm soapy water and a soft bristled brush to remove grime, sticky handprints and bird poo.

Paved areas

Paved areas should be swept regularly with a stiff heavy-duty broom. Don't hose them! It's not only illegal in areas with water restrictions; it can cause moss to grow on the surface. If you do have moss on your pavers, add a handful of salt to a solution of five parts water and one part vinegar. Paint it onto the moss, allow it to dry then sweep it off. Another solution is to spray the area with a mixture of one part vinegar and one part methylated spirits.

Outdoor rules

Drains, gutters and downpipes should be cleared regularly of leaves, pet hair and debris, hard areas should be swept, canvas chairs and umbrellas stored out of the weather to prevent rot and garden tools put away in the shed. (This also stops thieves using them to break in to your home.) Garden hoses should be stored on a reel to prevent them forming kinks or knots and keep them neatly out of the way when not in use.

Swimming pools

Swimming pools aren't the environmental enemies many people think they are. Maintained properly, the use of chemicals and electric vacuums can be minimised – as can the amount of water needed for top-ups. Tiles can be cleaned with a little bicarb on a soft cloth. Keep leaves out of the water by ensuring there are no trees overhanging the pool and keep a small tub filled with some pool water next to the stairs so swimmers can wash their feet before jumping in. Cover the pool when it's not in use and use a hand-held skimmer to remove leaves from the surface before they sink to the bottom. (That way you minimise the need to use the electric pool vacuum.) Run the filter for a few hours every day (consider putting it on a timer) rather than allowing dirt and debris to build up. Check the chemical balance of the pool water daily and treat immediately – this prevents problems building up and the need for expensive repairs. The overall message is – clean little and often, and don't be afraid to use the manual cleaning tools!

Outdoor stains

Save yourself a lot of effort (and the temptation to reach for a heavy duty chemical cleaner) by treating outdoor stains and spills straight away. Sprinkle cat litter over oil or grease on concrete or pavers. When the liquid is absorbed, sweep it up. (And tell you son to get his old bomb fixed!) When the barbie's over, and the embarrassing rellies have gone, clear up the greasy spills by combining equal amounts of fuller's earth and bicarb with enough water to make a wet paste. Spread it over the stains and allow it to dry. Sweep up the residue and make a mental note not to volunteer to host the next family reunion! Stains on concrete, bricks or pavers can be cleaned with a solution of one tablespoon of borax in a litre of hot water.

Composting

Why not use all that green cleaning power you've embraced to help green the planet? Making compost can be heaps (pardon the pun) of fun, especially if you get the kids involved – and it doesn't need to take up a lot of room. The three bin system is probably the best, and it doesn't matter how big or small it is. (You could even try some old plastic tubs with holes drilled in the sides to allow the compost to 'breathe'.) Basically all you have to do is put food scraps (except meat and oil) in the first bin, as well as shredded newspaper and lawn clippings and household dust. (You'll need to add a bit of ready-made compost to the mix to get it started.) After a few weeks, move it to the second bin (this turns and airs it) and finally, after a few more weeks, move it to the third bin. Pretty soon you'll have turned mess into mulch.

Garage

Store chemicals in labelled containers, well out of the reach of children. Avoid synthetic garden chemicals, but remember that organic alternatives can still be dangerous if swallowed and should be stored out of the reach of children. Sweep the floor regularly and store everything up out of the way so you won't put off doing it!

The car

Clean battery terminals with a mixture of two teaspoons of bicarb and one litre of water. Smear petroleum jelly around the base of the terminals to prevent further build-up. Wash the car and allow it to dry then sprinkle with cornflour and polish with a soft cloth. Polish chrome with bicarb and a soft dry cloth. Remove tar with eucalyptus oil. Wipe vinyl surfaces with a white vinegar and warm water solution, then air well. (This gets rid of that new car smell we all love, but which is actually harmful VOCs being released into the air.) Clean windows with a soft cloth moistened with vinegar. Place an open container of bicarb in the car to remove doggy or cigarette smells. There are also waterless car wash cleaners available. And if you don't want to do it yourself, call one of the eco carwash companies on the net.

Organic bug sprays

Why pay a fortune for something that makes your vegies inedible and your flowers stink? Home-made pest sprays are natural, safe, environmentally-friendly and won't cost you the earth. Just remember that not all creepy crawlies are the enemy. Ladybugs, praying mantis, lacewings, spiders and horsehair snakes are just some of the little creatures you should be making friends with in the garden. (No, we don't recommend cuddling a tarantula, just let him do his job!) These guys eat the nasty little bugs that like nothing more than feasting on your flowers and vegies. If the nasties out number the good guys, try one of the following home-made remedies.

Alcohol spray

This is just one of several home-made sprays guaranteed to ruin the party for aphids, mealy bugs, scale insects, thrips and whiteflies. Alcohol can damage some plants, such as African violets and apple trees, but can be used on plants with heavy, waxy leaves that won't be easily burned. It pays to do a test spray on a few leaves first then wait a few days to ensure the solution won't destroy the plant. So how do you make it? Simple. Mix one or two cups of 70 per cent rubbing alcohol with a litre of water, pop it in a spray bottle and away you go!

Tomato leaf spray

Plants like tomatoes and potatoes have water-soluble toxic compounds in their leaves that don't kill the enemy, but call in reinforcements to do the job instead. Put simply, the good bugs follow the smell of the spray, see the bad guys and gobble them up. Use it to protect plants from aphids by soaking one or two cups of chopped tomato (or spud) leaves overnight in two cups of water. Strain through cheesecloth or fine mesh, add another two cups of water and spray it wherever those pesky aphids are partying!

Garlic oil spray

It may kill off any romantic thoughts your plants were having, but garlic will also destroy pests such as aphids, earwigs, leafhoppers and whiteflies. Just soak 100 g of minced garlic cloves in two teaspoons of oil for 24 hours. Add half a litre of water mixed with a squirt of dishwashing liquid, stir thoroughly and strain into a glass jar for storage. When you want to use it, dilute one or two tablespoons in half a litre of water and spray away. (Don't forget to do a test spray on a few leaves first.)

Herbal sprays

Aromatic herbs may smell great to us – but garden pests hate them. Try sprays made from sage, thyme and rosemary to prevent caterpillar damage on cabbages, nasturtium tea to protect fruit trees from aphids, and catnip, chive or marigold solutions to stop most leaf-eating pests. Just mash one or two cups of fresh leaves with two to four cups of water and allow them to soak overnight. Strain the solution through cheesecloth, dilute with another two to four cups of water and a squirt of liquid soap then spray to your heart's content.

Hot dusts

Why don't ants eat out in Mexican restaurants? Because they can't stand chilli. Or black pepper, dill, ginger and paprika come to mention it. Hot dusts sprinkled around the base of plants repel ants, which often protect aphid colonies on plants. Just grind up the ingredient of your choice in a mortar and pestle and sprinkle around onions, carrots and cabbages in the vegie patch, as well as around the base of plants that tend to be attacked by aphids.

Pyrethrin

So you thought daisies were pretty little flowers that wouldn't harm a fly. Wrong! These innocent little flowers won't just harm a fly; they'll knock 'em dead! Not to mention aphids, stink bugs, thrips, tomato pinworms, whiteflies, gnats and mosquitoes. Grow your own pyrethrum daisies in the garden, enjoy the flowers and pick a few in full bloom. Hang the flowers in a dark, sheltered spot to dry, then grind them to a fine powder with a mortar and pestle. Mix with water and store in a glass jar. Spray on plants in the early evening (pyrethrin works best in cooler temperatures) and be very careful to use it near ponds and waterways as it is toxic to fish and aquatic insects.

Pot luck

Clean flowerpots, whether they are plastic, glazed or unglazed clay, ceramic or other materials with a solution made from one cup of white vinegar, one cup of methylated spirits, one cup of water and three drops of dishwashing liquid. Mix the ingredients together in a spray bottle, spray on the pot's surface, then scrub. If you'd prefer to avoid scrubbing, soak the pots for about an hour in a solution of two parts water to one part white vinegar. Any algae or mineral deposits should then simply rinse off.

Notes